JADEN
Smith

by Golriz Golkar

CAPSTONE PRESS
a capstone imprint

Bright Idea Books are published by Capstone Press
1710 Roe Crest Drive, North Mankato, Minnesota 56003
www.mycapstone.com

Library of Congress Cataloging-in-Publication Data
Names: Golkar, Golriz, author.
Title: Jaden Smith / by Golriz Golkar.
Description: North Mankato, Minnesota : Bright Idea Books, [2019] | Series:
   Influential people | Includes bibliographical references and index.
Identifiers: LCCN 2018019499 (print) | LCCN 2018025445 (ebook) | ISBN
   9781543541731 (ebook) | ISBN 9781543541335 (hardcover : alk. paper)
Subjects: LCSH: Smith, Jaden, 1998---Juvenile literature. | Actors--United
   States--Biography--Juvenile literature.
Classification: LCC PN2287.S6125 (ebook) | LCC PN2287.S6125 G665 2019 (print)
   | DDC 791.4302/8092 [B] --dc23
LC record available at https://lccn.loc.gov/2018019499

Editorial Credits
Editor: Mirella Miller
Designer: Becky Daum
Production Specialist: Megan Ellis

Photo Credits
AP Images: Jordan Strauss/Invision, cover; Newscom: Abaca Press/Hahn Lionel/Abaca/Sipa USA,
20, Columbia Pictures/Album, 6, Dafydd Owen/Retna/Photoshot, 18–19, Keizo Mori/UPI, 12–13,
Lucy Nicholson/Reuters, 17, MHD/PacificCoastNews, 23, Overbook Entertainment/Escape Artists/
Columbia Pictures Corp/Zade Rosenthal/Album, 9; Rex Features: Chelsea Lauren/Variety, 24–25;
Shutterstock Images: 360b, 14–15, DFree, 10–11, 28, Joe Seer, 5, Kathy Hutchins, 26–27,
Rawpixel.com, 31

Design Elements: iStockphoto, Red Line Editorial, and Shutterstock Images

TABLE OF CONTENTS

CHAPTER 1

A YOUNG
Movie Star

The fans cheered. Photographers snapped pictures. Jaden Smith had arrived with his family. He waved and smiled on the red carpet. He posed for pictures with fans. He spoke to reporters.

Smith was at a movie **premiere** in 2010. The movie *The Karate Kid* was opening. Smith was the star. People loved his acting. They admired his karate moves.

Smith posed on the red carpet for the premiere of his new movie.

Smith did his own stunts and moves in *The Karate Kid*.

The movie was a hit. It was not Smith's first role. But it made him a star. He had already been in two other movies. And he was only 11 years old!

LEARNING KARATE

Smith learned karate for *The Karate Kid*. He learned it in just a few months!

LIKE FATHER, LIKE SON

Will Smith was making a new movie in 2006. The movie was *The Pursuit of Happyness*. It was about a father and son. Someone needed to play the son. Smith's son Jaden was the perfect choice. He was 8 years old. This was his first movie role.

The movie was successful. Everyone loved Jaden Smith's acting. He won an award in 2007. Soon he played guest roles on TV. It was the start of his acting career.

Smith and his father in
The Pursuit of Happyness

CHAPTER 2

A FAMOUS
Family

Smith was born in California. He grew up with his parents and sister. His father, Will Smith, is an actor and rapper. His mother, Jada Pinkett Smith, is an actress.

The Smith family attended a movie premiere in Los Angeles, California.

11

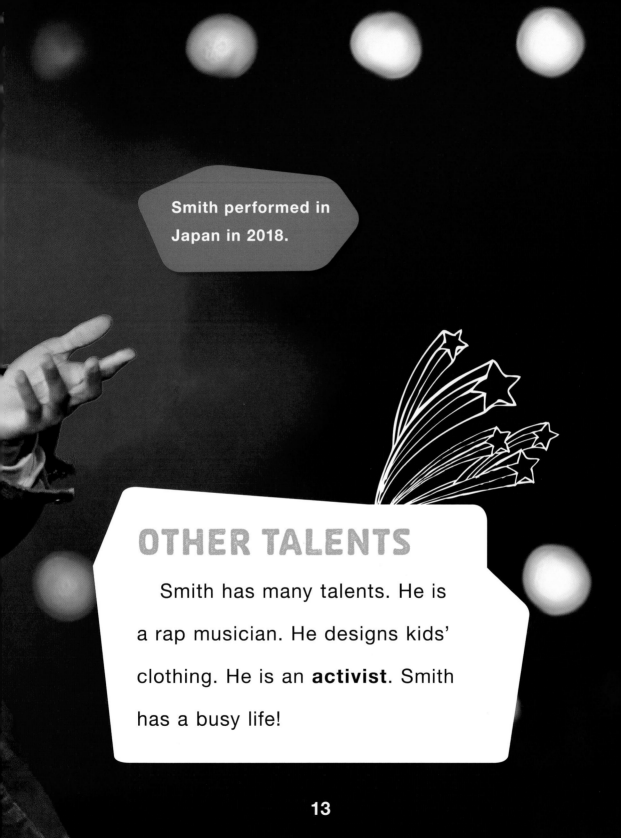

Smith performed in Japan in 2018.

OTHER TALENTS

Smith has many talents. He is a rap musician. He designs kids' clothing. He is an **activist**. Smith has a busy life!

Smith's parents taught him to help others. He gave kids in Africa clothes and toys. He enjoyed helping people.

CHAPTER 3

MUSICAL
Interests

Smith also likes making rap music. It helps him voice his feelings. He speaks his mind freely. His friend Justin Bieber is a singer. Bieber asked to sing with Smith. They recorded a hit song in 2010.

Smith and Bieber performed at the Grammy Awards in 2011.

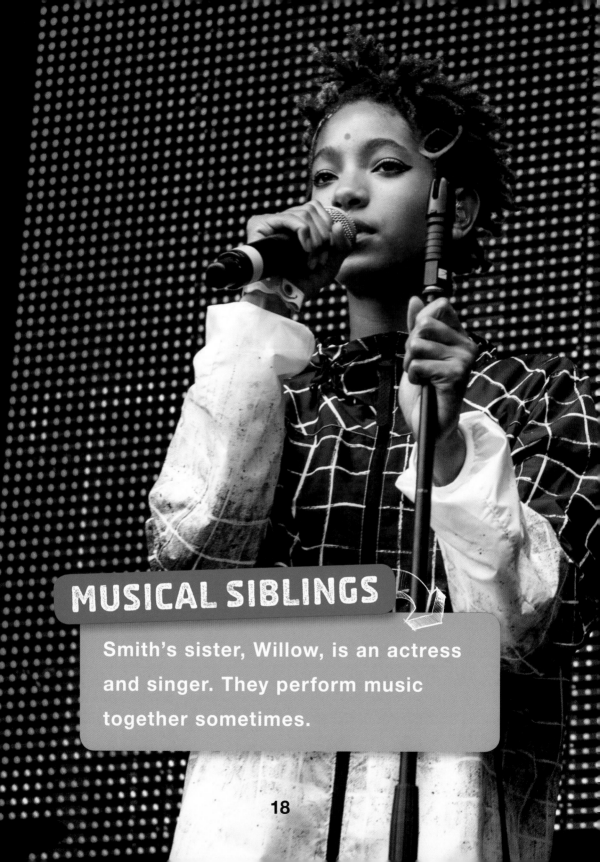

MUSICAL SIBLINGS

Smith's sister, Willow, is an actress and singer. They perform music together sometimes.

Smith wanted to make more music. He made a **mixtape** in 2012. Songs by other artists inspired it.

Smith and his sister, Willow, performed in London, England, in 2015.

Smith sang
for a crowd in
February 2018.

HIS OWN ALBUM

Smith decided to make his own album in 2017. He wanted to express his own ideas. A record company produced it. It received good reviews once it was released. People thought it was creative. It mixed rap and hip-hop music. Smith sang about **social inequality**. He also sang about his life.

CHAPTER 4

AN OUTSPOKEN
Celebrity

Smith also loves fashion. He created his own clothing company in 2016. The clothing is designed for any **gender**. Both boys and girls can wear it. He wants kids to feel confident in their clothing.

FASHION COMPANY

Smith's fashion company is MSFTS. The name comes from the word "misfits."

Smith (right) posed with friends in pieces from his clothing line.

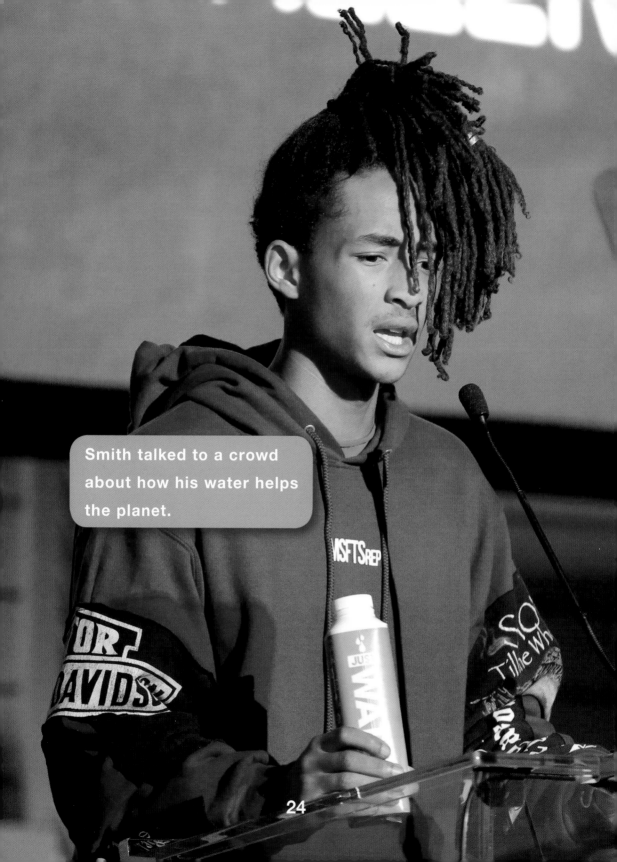

Smith talked to a crowd about how his water helps the planet.

HELPING THE EARTH

Smith cares about the environment. He wants to take action to help our planet. He created a water brand. It is called JUST Water. The cartons use materials that are safe for our planet. Smith won an environmental award in 2016. But Smith has more plans. He wants to do more for the planet. He wants people in Africa to have clean water.

26

Smith continues to act and make music. He is also an activist. He helps people in Africa by getting them food and medicine.

Smith has many talents. He entertains us with his movies. He impresses us with his music. He tells us to speak our minds. And he inspires us to help the world.

GLOSSARY

activist
a person who supports
a specific cause in an
outspoken way

gender
a person's identity as male,
female, or as neither male
or female

mixtape
a compilation of music
inspired or produced
by different artists

premiere
the first public performance
or showing of a movie or
theater production

social inequality
unequal wealth or
opportunities for specific
groups of people in society

28

TIMELINE

1998: Jaden Smith is born in Malibu, California.

2006: He stars in his first movie, *The Pursuit of Happyness*.

2010: He teams up with Justin Bieber on the hit song "Never Say Never."

2012: He releases his first mixtape, *The Cool Cafe*.

2016: He begins his clothing line, MSFTS.

2016: He wins an EMA Award for his work with the JUST Water company.

2017: He releases his first rap album, *Syre*.

ACTIVITY

MAKE A MUSIC VIDEO

Jaden Smith has made many movies, but he has also made many music videos. Think of a song you and your friends like. If you want, you can even write your own song! Create a music video together by singing and acting out the song while the music plays. Wear fun costumes and use props to help you.

FURTHER RESOURCES

Love learning about Jaden Smith? Learn more here:

Jaden Smith Fun Facts
http://www.kidzworld.com/article/28254-jaden-smith-fun-facts

Rajczak, Kristen. *Jaden Smith*. New York: Gareth Stevens, 2012.

Schwartz, Heather E. *Jaden Smith: Actor, Rapper, and Activist*.
    Minneapolis, Minn.: Lerner Publications, 2014.

**Want to get involved in acting or activism?
Check out these resources:**

Dias, Marley. *Marley Dias Gets It Done: And So Can You!* New York:
    Scholastic, 2018.

How to Become an Actor
https://www.learnhowtobecome.org/actor-or-actress/

INDEX